Traveling Makes You Smarter

Poems and Illustrations
by Aaron Brossoit

Copyright © 2012 Aaron Brossoit
Minneapolis, U.S.A.

All rights reserved. No part of this book may be used or reproduced in any manner whatsoever without written permission from the author.
For information contact brossoit@gmail.com.

Trade ISBN: 978-0615741475

Dedicated in loving memory
to my father
Mark A. Brossoit

Table of Contents

Traveling Makes You Smarter	2
Guy In A Tree	4
Might	6
Time Flies	8
Growly Thing	10
You Should Always Play Music	12
Three-toed Sloth	14
Opportunity Blues	16
Nose Between My Toes	18
Food Versus Time	20
Worry	22
So Many Places	24
Astronaut	26
Bass Man	28
A Feat of Cats	30
Stuck	32
String	34
Horrible Terrible Land of the Dead	36
Ghost Pepper	38
Sand	40
Twisty Twins	42
Favorite Music	44
Juggle	46
Digital Divide	48
Too Many Cats	50
Satellite	52
Kingdom	54
Snake Keeper	56
There	58
Button	60

Traveling Makes You Smarter

Traveling makes you smarter
'cause you see so many places.
There is nothing in a text book
that replaces foreign faces.

When you do you'll surely see
each culture has a history
and much more similarity
you didn't see
previously.

Traveling makes you smarter
'cause there is learning that's not read.
Smells and sounds of foreign towns
make memories in your head.

It is outside your comfort zone
that traveling makes you realize
the life you have is glamorous
in many other people's eyes.

So if you get that feeling
that life is getting harder
that things are lame...
and all the same...

Traveling makes you smarter.

Guy In A Tree

I once knew a guy who
sat high in a tree.
He wouldn't come down
and talk to me.

I waited all day and
I waited all night
and figured that when
the time was right

When he thought no one
would be around,
he'd climb the branches
to the ground.

And then I could give him
another scare
'cause that is how
I got him up there.

Might

The pen is mightier than the sword
but that's not always right.
If the sword cuts the pen in half
before it gets to write.

Time Flies

They say time flies
when you're having fun.
But where does it go
when the fun is done?
When you have to do work
and the time it slows,
does it walk on the ground?
Is that where time goes?

Does fun give time wings?
Or maybe it floats
each minute and second
relaxing in boats.

And if time's having fun
does it think that fun flies?
When it's time to keep time
does the time think fun dies?

And although it's been fun
reading this rhyme,
it's here that it ends
'cause I haven't the time.

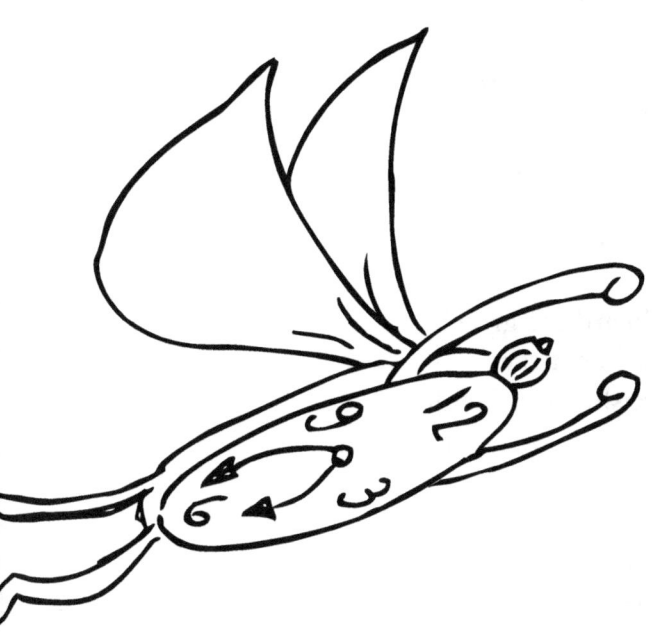

Growly Thing

I was hiking in the woods one eve
just after sun had set
and when I stopped to take a pee
the darkness growled back at me.
(I think my pants got wet)

Although I only heard the growl
I'm sure the thing was furry.
The teeth I bet are sharp and white
and in the dark it has good sight.
It gives me cause to worry.

I warned the other hikers but
they thought I was a liar.
There wasn't time to change their mind.
The growly thing was close behind.
I had to start a fire!

I ran to camp to make a fire
and huddled safely there.
Just in the dark behind a tree
the growly thing just stared at me
afraid to burn its hair.

Remembering that fearsome beast
is giving me the shakes.
Just don't forget that every night
when darkness swallows up the light
the growly thing awakes.

You Should Always Play Music

You should always play music
it's important for the soul.
Mastering an instrument
or drumming on a bowl.

Something we were born with
knows when the music's right,
and when you play with others
your soul turns on a light.

No matter what your language
or ability to see
by music we're connected
SPIRITUALLY.

Three-toed Sloth

If you ever meet a three-toed sloth
then you will surely see,
it travels very slow on land
but pretty quick by tree.

So in the end
you can't pretend
a sloth could lend
a helping hand.

A different friend
you'll need to send
to travel quickly
over land.

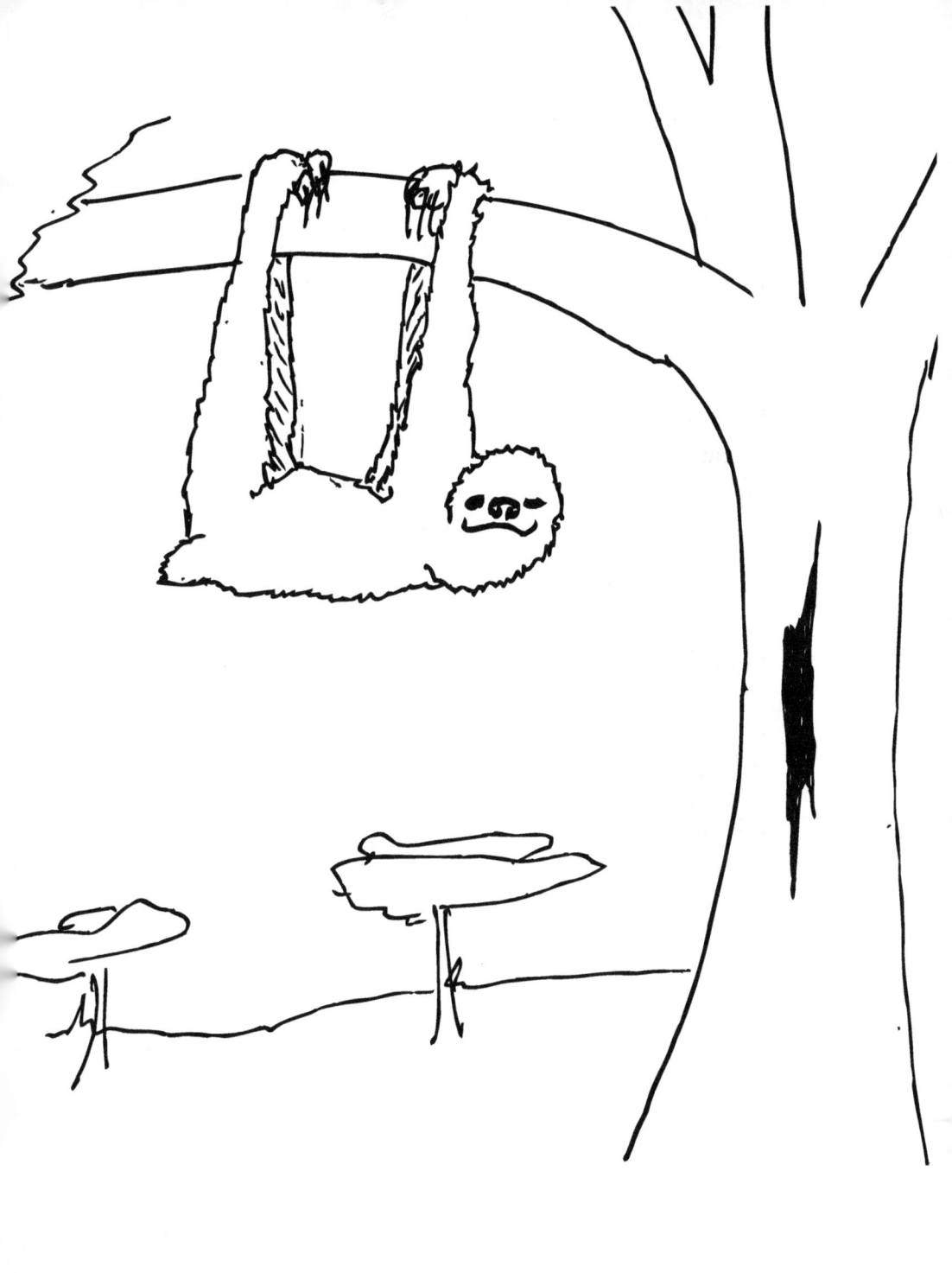

Opportunity Blues

When you are young
you may be told
to hold your tongue
or be strong and bold.

No matter the case
beware of the time
it maintains the pace
of a quickly read rhyme.

Opportunity
is the option to be
all you can be
in the land of the free.

But it is but a tock
on a grandfather clock
'though the grandfather's
no longer ticking.

Nose Between My Toes

There's a nose that grows
between my toes.

It slowly grows
between the rows.

And when it snows,
the nose it blows

and snot it flows
between my toes.

Eeeeewwwww!

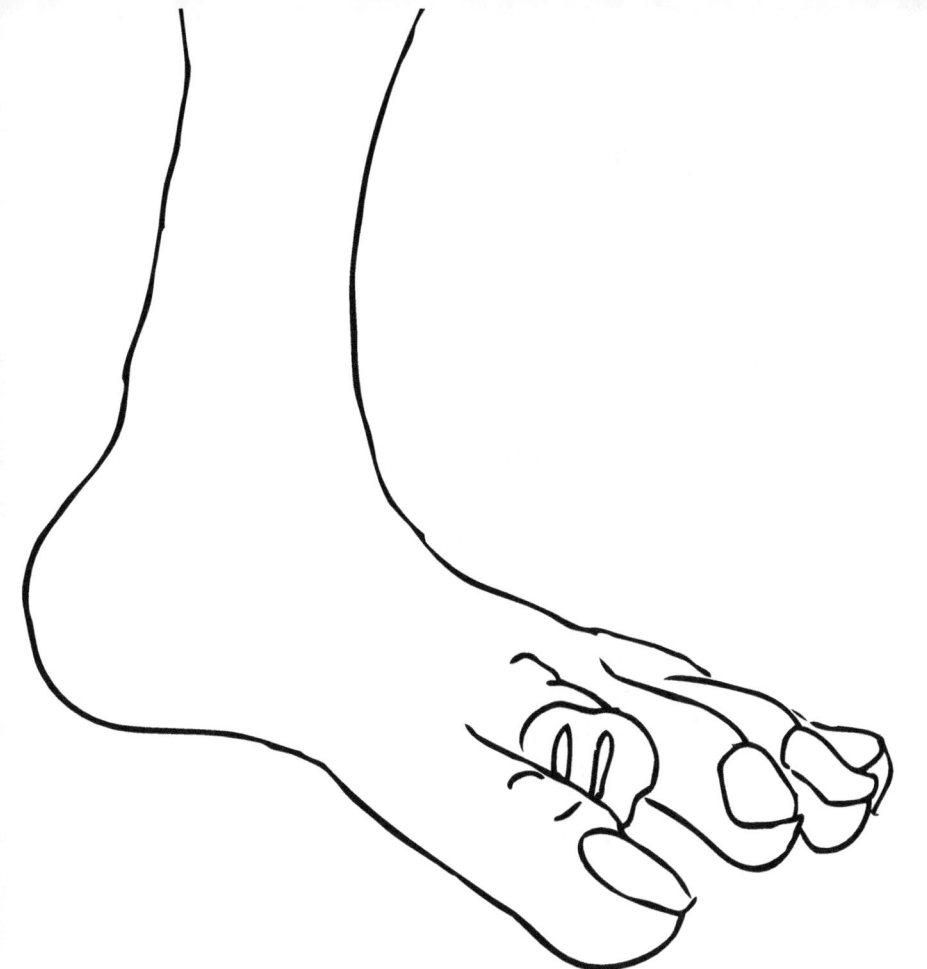

Food Versus Time

If you didn't have to eat
you'd save a lot of time.
Each day instead you'd take a pill
just larger than a dime.

Breakfast you could always skip
and sleep an hour late,
and every lunch you'd have the time
no need to leave work late.

And since dinner comes much thinner
you could stay out having fun.
Instead of feasting every night
the tasks would all be done.

But when I think of food I love
I'm filled with sentiment.
No matter how much time I saved
eating food is time well spent.

<u>Worry</u>

There is no point to worrying.
It's all up in your head.
Each moment you spend doing it,
you miss your life instead.

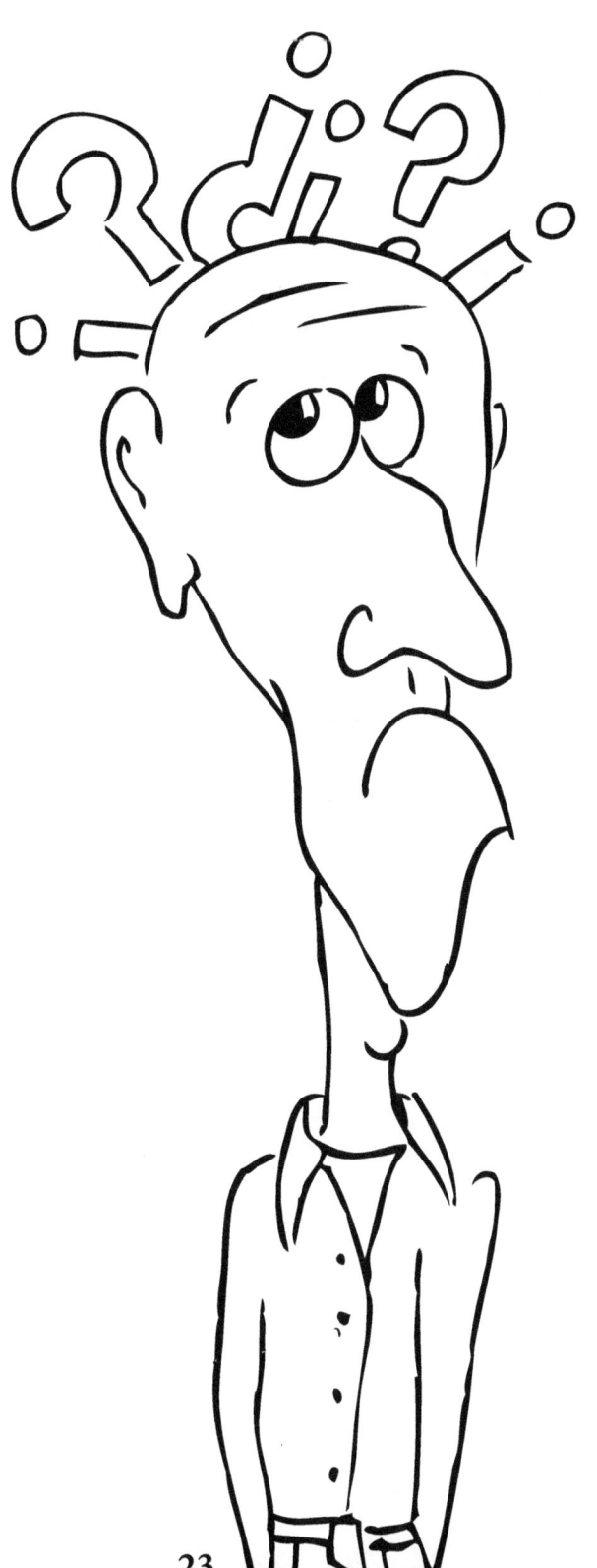

So Many Places

There are so many places to visit
I don't know where to go.

There are so many things to learn
I don't know what to know.

There are so many songs to hear
I don't know what to play.

So many things to remember
every single day.

Just go somewhere soon
and learn something fast,
play the next tune
live each day as your last!

Astronaut

I wanted to be an astronaut.
My mom thought that was cute
so I bought some parts and glue
and made myself a suit.

I worked all day and worked all night
to make sure that it fit me right.
But now that it is getting hot
I'm stuck inside an astronaut.

Bass Man

Hats off to the bass man
he keeps that funky groove.
Fingers walking on the neck
he makes the music move.

Let's hear it for the drummer
holding down the beat
tapping, brushing cymbals,
a bass drum at his feet.

The singer's dress, it sparkles.
She sings a loungy song.
Her voice it fills the darkened room.
Each word she sings is drawn out long.

Whoever is playing piano
I hope will leave stage soon.
This music sounds atrocious
with the piano out of tune.

A Feat of Cats

A cat can land upon its feet
from many stories high.

That's something that you ought to know
but shouldn't ever try.

Stuck

I'm sick and tired of
feeling sick.
I'm stuck in the mud
being a stick.
I'm under the weather
feeling rain.
I'm under the wear
being a stain.
I'm feeling bored with
so much to do.
So many colors
but feeling blue.
It all looks like dirt
'cause my head's in the sand.
My horn's out of tune
as I play in the band.

But I'm sick of the stick!
I'll rain on that stain!
The blue just won't do
and the band, it's a pain!

I'll adventure outside and
find something to do,
open my mind and
expect something new.

String

Whenever I go on a hike
I often do this thing,
behind my every step,
I leave a trail of string.

That way I can be worry free
wherever I may roam.
If it gets dark or I take a wrong turn
I can follow the string back home.

But currently,
I seem to be
in a jam
I did not forsee…

It's hard to unravel your travel
after climbing a tree.

Horrible Terrible Land of the Dead

The horrible terrible land of the dead,
I thought the place was all in my head.
At least that's what the doctor said
of the horrible terrible land of the dead.

The horrible terrible land of the dead,
turns out the place was under my bed!
What a terrible smell, a big hole glowing red
in the horrible terrible land of the dead.

The horrible terrible land of the dead,
isn't as bad as I previously said.
The people were nice! I left happy and fed
in the horrible terrible land of the dead.

Ghost Pepper

There is a pepper in the fridge
it haunts me day and night.
When I reach to grab a condiment
it gives me quite a fright!

It looks just like a pepper
that I would love to eat,
but the world's spiciest pepper
is a little too much heat.

Sand

Sitting on a beach
a thought did come to pass
that I could heat the sand below
and melt it into glass,

Then shape the glass into a bowl
and pour some sand inside.
The sand expands to fill the space
 completely tall and wide.

Now think about your thoughts
as small pieces of sand
Consider that you shape the glass
that keeps you where you stand.

Twisty Twins

The twisty twins did
a terrific trick
with a couple spins
they were tangled up thick!

With the bend of a leg
and the crack of a joint
the audience gasped,
"This did not disappoint!"

With the tuck of an arm
(or more so a torso)
they folded and molded
but that's not the worse though.

They twisted and twisted up into a ball
twisted until there was nothing at all!

"An amazing trick!"
the audience cheered
but forever the twins
had disappeared.

Favorite Music

What's your favorite music type
a friend will surely ask.
But answering that question
is no simplistic task.

Do they mean your favorite music type
while listening alone?
Or favorite type to listen to
holding on a phone?

Do they mean your favorite music type
to dance and shake your hips?
Or music that you like to hear
when kissing someone's lips?

But no one wants to hear you say
that you like everything
so choose the type of music
that you wish that you could sing!

Juggle

If I could remember a million things
and juggle a million balls
I'd handle a million problems
while taking a million calls,
and answer a million questions
a million times each date.
But I can't remember a million things,

I can only remember eight.

Digital Divide

I'm not going to learn at all.
I'll find it all online.
I won't remember directions
or names of friends of mine.

I'll trust that my computers
will lead the proper way
and always be surprised
when I find myself astray.

I no longer need to read
or think about the past.
The news comes at a speed
where the meaning doesn't last.

But then I catch a glimpse outside,
the sun it makes me smile wide.
It's time to visit the other side
of the digital divide.

Under that enormous sky
connected life becomes.
It reminds me of our ancestry
the primal beat of drums.

It's there I find my critic torn
and yearn to learn about the past,
in hopes new stories will be born
not just the same webcast.

Too Many Cats

First I bought an orange cat
then a brown one too.
Then I met a calico and
found a persian blue.

The white one came from a friend,
who sneezed from all its hair.
There's a litter of little fuzzy ones
napping in the chair.

The fat cat, the striped cat,
the cat with no tail
arrived yesterday
in a box in the mail.

The grey one, the black one
and seven cats more
were meowing this morning
outside my front door.

So now that I have a house full of cats
there's only one thing to be done,
sit on the couch with them all in my lap
and take a cat nap in the sun.

Satellite

Do you ever get that feeling
that someone's watching you?
No matter where you go
they see the things you do?

That feeling in the starry night
that there may be a satellite
that points a camera at the ground
and always follows you around?

And everything you say is heard,
they analyze your every word
to see if it is really true
that someone who is just like you,
will do the things they say they'll do
or say they'll do but not come true.

But that's just a conspiracy.
The one who's watching you...

IS ME!

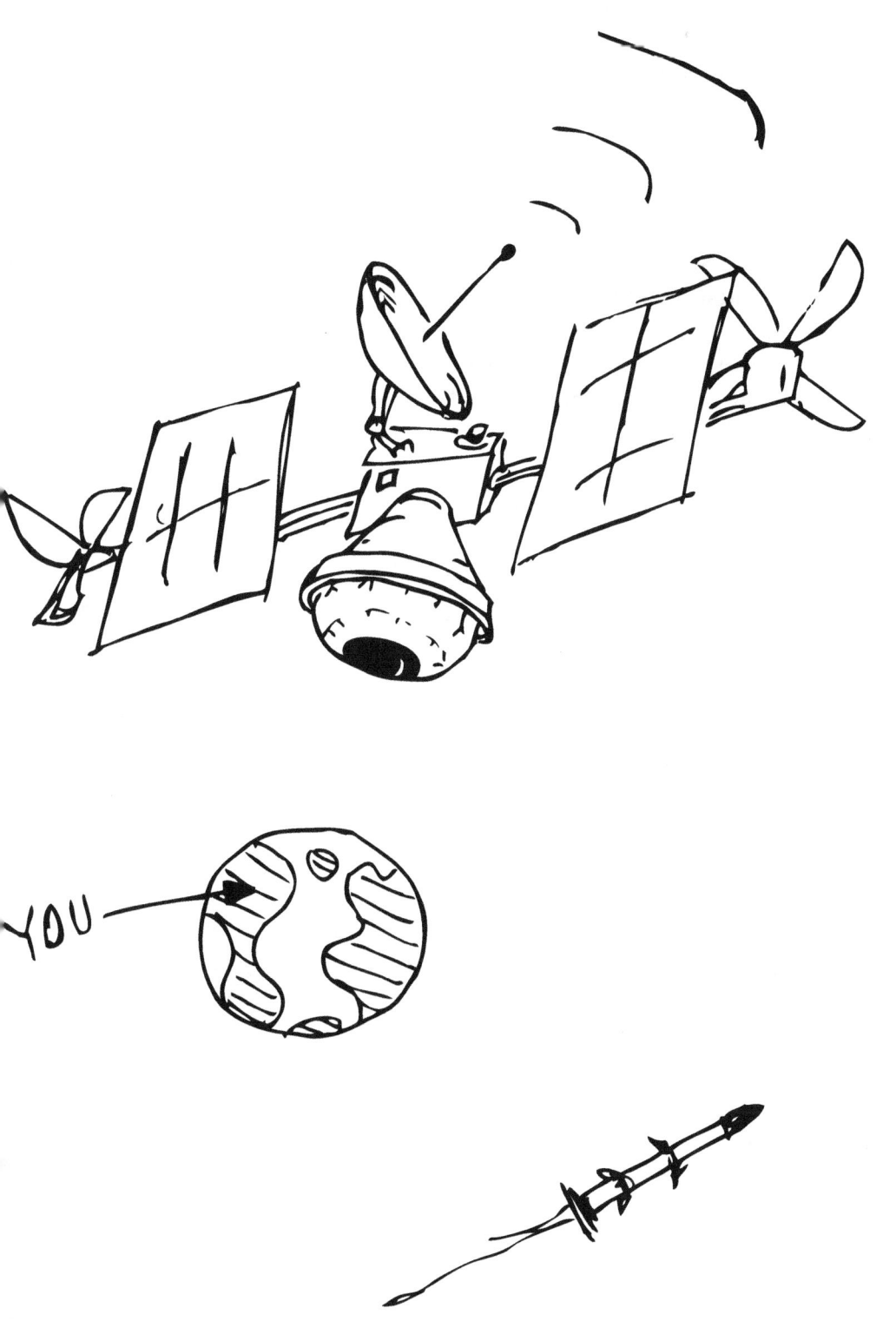

Kingdom

I am the king of this land
it has everything I want.

A castle, a river, a town full of homes
and a fancy restaurant.

The people that live here love me so much,
they made me king of this land

'cause I can build whatever they want
in a sandbox full of sand.

Snake Keeper

I've worked at the zoo for 82 years
cleaning the cages of snakes.

But now that I've retired
I have uncontrollable shakes.

There

I can travel by foot or by bike or plane
through sand or grass or snow.
But I can't get away from here
no matter where I go.

I can stand right here
and look over there
and clearly see
where I want to be…

But once I am there,
the there becomes here
and the here where I was
becomes there!

Button

There is a button on my wall.
I don't know what it's for.
Perhaps it opens up a door
that's hidden in the floor?

There is a button on my wall.
It's one I've never seen.
Do you think it starts a strange machine?
Does it turn the sky from blue to green?

There is a button on my wall.
It's shiny and it's red.
I remember what my father said,
"You must take risks to get ahead!"

Click

Aaaaaaaaahhhhhh!!!

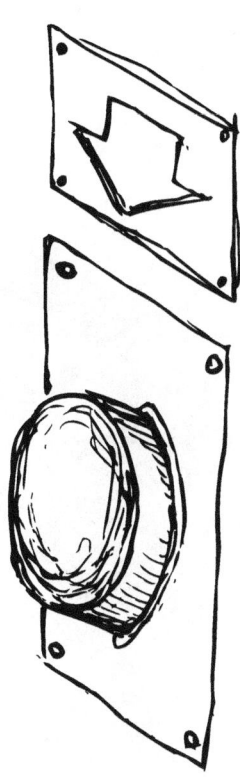

ABOUT THE AUTHOR

Aaron Brossoit is a Minnesota-based poet and illustrator. He lives with his wife and two cats and is incredibly handsome... and modest. He also writes about himself in third person. His favorite number is 82. (Do you remember what poem it was in?)

In first person:
Special thanks to my wife Angel, my Mother, all my nieces and nephews and Samuel Elsworth Kiser for inspiration and support.

www.ingramcontent.com/pod-product-compliance
Lightning Source LLC
Chambersburg PA
CBHW061511040426
42450CB00008B/1570